INK VEINS

I0380684

PERSEPHONE AUTUMN

bashful heart

Protected, guarded
Sheltered from days past
Peeking from the shadows
Speeding, pulsing too fast
Timid by design
Receipt of youth's elements
Shaping new pieces
For life's puzzling moments
Bashful heart
Step out of your shell
Worry not of rejection
For you can compel
Brave as a lioness
Composure so strong
Expose your beautiful heart
As it sings its soulful song

World Less Traveled

Walking the path
A place untraveled
Taken aback by beauty
A new world unraveled
Air fresh, crisp in my quest
Eyes alive, seeking behest
Exploring and searching
Destinations unknown
Memories of a life
I'd like to call home
Dig up your ambition
Bring forward your dreams
Where you want to be
Never as far as it seems

Stranger in my Skin

Stranger
My body a foreign space

Uncomfortable
My skin and curves all wrong

Awkward
Unable to comprehend my own beauty

Introversion
Not wanting to speak words at all

Be Beautiful

The amount of pigmentation your skin holds
makes you beautiful
Your gender, genetically given or transitioned,
makes you beautiful
Believing in something more than yourself
makes you beautiful
Loving another human wholeheartedly,
regardless of appearance, gender, or beliefs,
makes you beautiful
Standing up for what is moral and just
makes you beautiful
Spreading love, peace, and joy
makes you beautiful
Lifting others up
makes you beautiful
Being a voice for those who cannot use theirs
makes you beautiful
Striving for a healthier, more abundant planet
for future generations
makes you beautiful
Be strong
Be bold
Be unique
Be heard
Be loud
Be beautiful

Duality

What is it like
To live two lives
One sheltered
One coated in lies
Which is which
Who is who
Unending questions
Reality askew
What to believe
Unknown anymore
What you have seen, heard
Has happened before
Sugar coated words
Slipping from the cracks
Gone are the days
Of when you were not last
Only once in life
To feel great importance
Washed away with the tide
Left only by hindrance

Dance in the Rain

Wash away your woes
Feel freedom from your fears
Dance amongst the raindrops
Let the sky cry its tears
Open up yourself
Allow joy to flow
Have a carefree heart
Embrace the love you know
For dancing in the rain
Releases all your burdens
Brings your soul elation
Everything it yearns

Silhouette

Silhouette
A woman gone
Vanished from sight
Absent all along
Blurred visions
Distant thoughts
Fading from light
Into the depths of dark
Deep breath
Long sigh
Is it a memory
Or a dream gone awry

REAPER

She walks the Earth
Wings of black
Seeking the souls
No longer intact
Some so young
Many dear elder
Stealing their pain
Leaving none to suffer
A simple embrace
All she gives
Absorbing a life before
For those to relive

Stalker

Dark storm clouds
Following unbidden
A sole shadow
Pursuer in the night
No escape
Life of fear
Surrounded, enclosed
Paranoia appears
Stolen sight
Suffocation
Torn flesh
Goodbye…

Heart's Melody

Her heart strummed
As if lyrics in a song
First verse poetic
The chorus quite strong
Rhythm in harmony
Tempo just right
A song for satyrs
Each and every night
She wished for a melody
Fiercely to come alive
To hide all her weakness
Deep down inside

Battered Soul

Torn, beaten
Battered soul
Shed no tears
You have control
Life's journey
So many paths
Find your way
Be home at last
Life has one meaning
Love and happiness
Be who you are
Find your bliss

Soul of an Angel

Created from timeless beauty
Adored by endless love
Inside the cocoon of her mind
Behold answers from above
Embraced from within
Deep and passionate soul
Heartfelt woes of the many
Attempt to abduct control
Although wrapped tightly
She slowly releases herself
Ever the graceful angel
Wings spread, invitation open

Loved

Sometimes life strikes us hard
Pushes boundaries, leaves a scar
Shreds our thoughts
Grabs our fears
Steals our courage
Creates a life full of tears
Finding your strength
A life threatening task
Deep within you
Reach down and grasp
Use your heart
And use your mind
You are deeply loved
This is not a lie

Chieftainess

Rhythmic beats pulsing
Chanting songs, legends
Souls dance by flame
Ancestors come defend us
Ceremony of the Gods
Stories passed down line
Rites bestow to youth
To carry on throughout time
Collapse and kiss the Earth
Extend and speak to the Sun
Breathe in the tree's breath
Nature and body become one
Crown adorned with feathers
Flesh protected in hide
Beloved by her people
For she loves her tribe

Meaning of Life

A glimpse upon the mountainscape
Running bare amongst the trees
Open heart, open mind
How the Earth puts me at ease
Sight of the weeping willow
Such melancholy elegance
Vibration of the mighty redwood
Makes my soul soar and dance
Reflections upon lake waters
Mirror life's answers, intent
Quest for placement, truth
Life's mystery revealed, sent
Our existence is quite simple
Peaceful as a mourning dove
Gather, listen closely
Life is all about love

Blessed is the Witch

Dancing and chanting
Circling the fire
Sky clad for the Goddess
Radiating peace, love, desire
Do unto others
As you want done unto you
Follow your heart
Intuition beats true
A handful of Earth
Chalice of water
Frankincense in the air
Spirit surrounds fire, slight totter
Gaze up at the stars
Feel the Earth down below
Blessed is the witch
Whose soul forever grows

Love and Light

Laced up and ready
Tap your heels thrice
No place like home
Although some do entice
Bring along your wand
Your censer, your staff
Merry meet, Merry part
Let us share love and a laugh
So dance with me
Throughout the night
Be one with nature
Embrace love and light

The Storm

Brewing

Churning

Sky lit

Burning

Roaring

Inching

Heavens open

Drenching

Awakened

Meaning

Heartfelt

Dreaming

Refreshed

Renewed

Life

Beauty in view

Often she wondered
If her heart had a song
One that only plays
Singing where you belong
Awakening your soul
Eliminating pain
Rejuvenating life
Where you had never been
Light and energy ignite
Song begins to play
Unexplained elation
Continual desire to stay
Embrace me with your arms
Touch me with your soul
Kiss me with utter passion
Wrap me in control

Heart Song

delicate soul

delicate
Yet stronger than steel

graceful
Unique in her beauty

elegant
In the sway of her hips

magnetic
Attraction reels you in

authentic
Unlike any other

generous
Giving all to everyone

loving
Purest of all traits

A Single Breath

Celebrations
All in good cheer
Bring others joy
Family, friends, or a peer
Be gracious, Be kind
Be full of heart
Touch someone's mind
Love life like an art
Thoughtful
Gentle beauty
Passionate
As one should be
A world through another's eyes
We all should see
Imagine the difference
Imagine the possibility
Take a moment
Just one deep breath
For everything amaze
Everything has depth

Undeniable

So delicate and soft
Like the petals of a rose
So fragrant and sweet
A delicacy to behold
With curves and thorns
Proceed with care
Both alluring and dangerous
Unknowing how you'll fair
Tempting the senses
Slowly one by one
You won't know what hit you
Suddenly you're undone
Petals open up
Unable to pull away
Drawn inches closer
No reason to stray
To see, to smell
Touch more desirable
Like satin or silk
Impulse undeniable

Path of Intuition

Shadowed trail
Treading without fear
Eyes open, searching
What is found here
Parts ever winding
Some straight and narrow
Will intuition guide
Will the path harrow
Patches of light
Sparking visions unknown
Fade into darkness
Hidden future left untold
Whispers and enchantments
Sounds filling the gaps
Unclear, indecipherable
Time in lapse
Mysterious, silent
Certainty unknown
Harboring what's close
Capturing your home

Mother Earth

Today I stared into the trees
I watched the leaves rustle by
Some green, some brown, and red
Some even floating in the sky

Nature has an irreversible beauty
Regardless to the raping of man
To know life forms and energy withstand
More than any one human can

To see the world diminish
Sadness pours from my eyes
For some to not understand
Can't you hear Nature's cries

Increased weather phenomenon
Nature will have her revenge
Respect Mother Earth's gifts
She will give us leverage

Birds and trees and honeybees
Squirrels and snakes and rabbits too
Sharing our world with all species
These are only a few

Thoughts of a Madwoman

Rivers and pools and streams everywhere
Constant feeling of not knowing
My heart flutters
It is nervous
Appealing to my desires
Movements, gestures, postures scream
Pulled in all directions of the mind
Sight all in red...
Desire, lust, pain, fear
Path on a twisted road
Tears of blood pouring out of my head
Images captured like photos in my memory
Wind, sand, oceans, fire
The thoughts of a mad woman
Challenged by life

Heart pounding
Breath unsteady
Extremities shaking
Mind whirling
Room constricting
Body punishing
Shutting down
Falling
Fading
Drifting
Gone

AnXiEtY

Once

Once
For a single breath in time
For a single beat of my heart
For one, lonely tear
Once
It isn't the world
It isn't my final breath
To some, meaningless
Others, everything
Searing
Scorching
Devotion
Life

Distraction

Days and nights
You beckon, you call
Needing and pining
Desire before all
We crave our words
Voices soothe the other
Continual contact
Connected to one another
Distractions float in
I am second in line
Who am I but a girl
You talk with time to time
Our connection is strong
Right now I feel weak
You've sucked the life force
Directly out of me
Don't pity my heart
We are where we are
But it hurts no less
Knowing a distraction pulls you far
It will all return
Your thoughts, focus align
When you're back to the norm
That is when you are mine
For now I sit
Mind wandering aimlessly
I need my own distraction
I need to just breathe

Days

Some days
The sun shines endlessly
Other days
The sky looms forever gray
Some days
Flowers bloom abundantly
Other days
Nothing but weeds
Some days
It is all you can eat
Other days
It is famine not feast
Some days
Smiles never die
Other days
Cheeks never dry
Some days
You want to never end
Other days
Life is a dead end
But alas
They are all just days

As I sit, stare, listen, observe
The world around me
Almost gone are the days of
Simplicity, ease, courtesy
Filtering in more
Concentrations of greed
Greed for what is not yours
Greed for what you cannot have
Greed for all things
Without rightfully earning
Quickly the days are fading
Of earning by hard labor
Replaced by twisted morality
Telling us we either
Work harder for less
Don't work and cheat to live
True appreciation slipping
Deep into the cracks
Cracks we cannot reach in
Cannot see its deep, dark pits
Vast and never ending
Reeks of hatred and jealousy
Pulsing with fear and dishonesty
But…

Society

Petals still bloom
Prisms ignite the sky
Rebirth follows blazes
Earth shifts, explodes
Forming new life, fascination
Resurrecting hope, beauty
Refreshing and replenishing
With only what is required
Eliminating non-essentials
Allowing us to begin anew
Treasuring values once lost
Breathing in beauty once ignored
Opportunity once more for…
Society

Land of Dreams

In the land of dreams
I am empowered
I am confident
I am outgoing

In the land of dreams
I am beautiful
I am radiant
I am desired

In the land of dreams
Optimism thrives
Pessimism is crushed
Generosity is abundant
Fear is diminished

In the land of dreams
Peace
Love
Elation

In the land of dreams…

Consumed

I walk the earth

Feet bare

Creating their own path

The breeze whips my hair

Yet

No air surrounds me

A plethora of colors

Blinded by distraction

Gathered

Absorbed

Dispersed

Consumed

Willfully taken

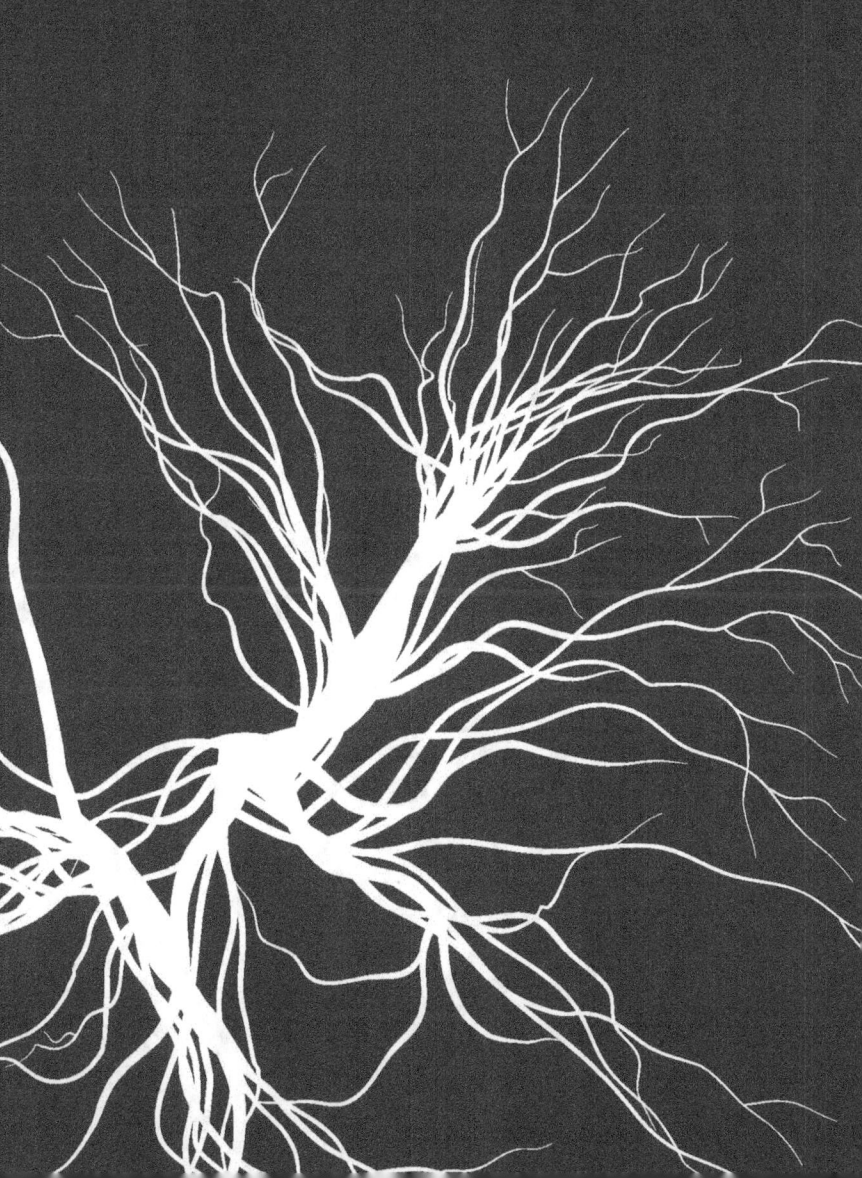

Inching closer
Surrounded by the sea
Inhabiting the space
Separating you from me
I reach out to touch
Reluctant, shy
Rejection a fear
But wishing to try
Acceptance amplified
Returned touch begins
Warmth spreads throughout
Bodies tremble within
Two sets of lips
Fragments apart
Merge into one
Anxiety laden heart
World fades, disappears
Your heart, all I hear
Breath forgotten
Lips, tongues subside
Exchange of hearts
Souls collide

When Souls Collide

Twin Flame

The woman I love
No words can compare
No words can describe
The love that we share
Her patience and passion
Amaze and astound
My savior, my world
Her beauty profound
My twin flame, destiny
She makes me whole
Awakening my heart
Awakening my soul
Life rings vibrant
With her by my side
Not soon enough
She will be my bride

Laying gently
Eyes fluttering
On the cusp of dreams
Mind all asunder
Vivid imagination
Running rampant
Heart pacing
Sweat beaded brow
Picturesque moment
Displayed internally
Swooning me
Pulling at my strings

cuddled whispers

Ecstasy

Heightened awareness
Tantalizing lips
Beckoning, yearning
For that deep slow kiss
Magnetic attraction
Like the weight of gravity
Tugs at my being
Desires in full clarity
Lips, tongues move slowly
Embracing in a dance
Inexplicable ecstasy
Two souls in a trance

I am Yours - You are Mine

Brought together
Braced as one
Magnetic pull
Never undone
Even at rest
Always entwined
I am yours
You are mine
Limbs that hook
Grab and squeeze
Always touch me
Yes and please

Bound for Eternity

Exquisite beauty
A gift beloved
Adorned in artistry
Below and above
Tears melt down
Pale cream cheeks
Love for her Master
He slowly speaks
"For you my pet
Are bound to me
Mind, body, and soul
For eternity"

Under the Stars

Brisk night air
Breeze light in passing
Starlit sky above
Soft field grass caressing
Gentle words spoken
Fingers stroke cheeks
Eyes close in trust
Lips touch for weeks
Time is lost, nonexistent
Consumed within touch
For this moment is eternal
We will never have enough
Fiery hands glide down
Seeking sides, hips
No star blazes so strong
As embracing your lips

Lover's Embrace

Something quite simple
A lover's embrace
Can melt your soul
Make your pulse race
Absence of woes
Diminished fears
Absolute trust
Passion that sears
No words need be spoken
Just lay next to me
Breathe in my essence
Capture every part of thee

Siren's Call

Run your toes
Across the keys
Play my melody
I beg you please
Your most beloved
Siren's call
Sing it for me
Watch me fall
No other tune
Steals my heart
Seals my soul
Keeps us apart

Fate is in Control

From depths unknown
A call so deep, profound
An undeniable pull
Heart's echo vibration, sound
No words need be spoken
Language all their own
Embracing one another
Their bodies the other's home
Enchanted by sensations
Overwhelmed wishing spell
Insatiable need, cravings
Only one can fulfill
Reaching, grabbing, pulling near
Voice of ancient love, whispering in your ear
Don't deny your heart, your body, your soul
Embrace your journey, trusting fate is in control

In two different worlds
Separated by planes
A wisp as you pass
Spirit erupts in my veins
My body trembles
Craves more from you
Deep in my bones
Passion continually grew
To tether and hold
Untouchable grasp
To feel your flesh
Undeniable ask
To see, to feel
To taste your being
Absorb all you are
Your every last meaning

Love Between Worlds

Immortal Love

Born from stardust
Rooted by Earth
Awoken by the gods
Showing their worth
Connected by energy
Intertwined, interlaced
Touch of flesh
First mortal embrace
Fingers tracing, learning
Path of constant tremble
Instinctual habits flourish
Mouths become nimble
Nature at the forefront
Passion to behold
Devouring one another
Creating love's mold

Wishes

Dreams are desires, wishes
Telling a story in your mind
Bringing forward smiles
Some end teary-eyed
Wishes of great passion
Wishes of an eternal kiss
Wishes of being touched
Everywhere with your lips
Desiring your warm skin
Grazing against mine
Hearts beat as one
Breaths, bodies merge like vine
Flesh and core
Symbiotic, as one
Dreams merge together
Wish granted, done

tangled lovers

To lay there
Still and unmoving
Wrapped with limbs
No words proving
Your breath in my ear
Mine on your neck
Heart beating under my palm
Should heating affect
Arms holding tightly
Replacing all worry
A kiss to the forehead
Love with no hurry
Embrace for an eternity
Soul quenching need
Fulfill one another
Nothing left to cede

Flesh

Flesh
Yours on mine
Warm and gentle
Soft, exquisite
Slow and supple
Freckled, smooth
Embracing
Kissing
Firmly holding
Not close enough
Intense
Deep
Passionate
Inseparable
One

My Cure

Wrap me up
Embrace me as yours
Hold me close
For your touch is my cure
Whisper sweet nothings
Invade me, heart and soul
Depths jolted alive
Tongue's infectious words control
Close your eyes
Imagine me there
Listen for my whispers
Whisper back if you dare

Imaginary Kiss

Eyes close, imagine
Your face before my own
A sigh leaves my lips
A feeling of home
I extend my hand
Caressing your cheek
Unable to resist
Our lips meet
Soft and slow
Passionate heat
Lips part, tongues tangle
Devouring so deep
Pulse soaring
Mind roams
Eyes open, awaken
Finding myself alone

Something so simple
Your chest against mine
Your breath in my ear
Pulses synced in time
Arms holding firm
Sliding into place
Friction heated bodies
Connected at the base
Movements slow and soft
Tempo aches to grow
Heightened kinetic energy
Backs begin to bow
Overwhelmed by sensation
Pulling from deep inside
Finding release together
Bound they will abide

Base
Connection

Unwavering

Lay down behind me
Your knee bent to mine
Wrap your hand around my waist
All our limbs intertwine
Your lips close to my ear
Whispering sweet words deeply
Of love and lust and forever
Filling me repletely
Twisting my body
I gaze into your eyes
Nothing fulfills me more
The wholeness your heart provides
Our lips graze softly
A taste of what is to come
Deep, heated passion
Only you make me undone
Heat and vigor
We are flesh to flesh
Hours become days
Never ending our famish
Impassioned for each other
Each the other's weakness
Unwavering love and lust
Achieving what completes us

Undeniable

A glance that makes you look away
An emotion that overwhelms your entire
body beyond comprehension
A thought that fascinates your mind
A desire for more than what is there
A drive to find what your soul needs
A touch that sends your mind to places it
has never been
A feeling so strong you cannot resist
A temptation completely undeniable

System Overload

Always in the eyes
They never lie
A touch of the hair
A caress of the skin
Subtle and sweet
A lean inward
Electric surge of emotion
System overload

Attraction

Often at night
As I lie in my bed
So many thoughts of you
Run through my head
Times we have shared
A smile crosses my face
Wishing you were next to me
So comforted by your embrace
Your perspective of me
The first I have ever known
Sharing so much of myself
So many ways I have grown
Any thought of empty time
When it doesn't involve you
I try to remain positive
Keep myself from becoming blue
The feelings that arise
When we are apart
A slow growing ache
Surrounding my heart
Deep feelings for you
Yearning always for more
Your deep feelings for me
I know them within my core
Our shared longing for one another
Like a love story from a book
The drive, the attraction, the lure
Love on a baited hook

Forever and ever.
Always

Written in the stars
Twin flames of a soul
Bound by the heart
Together we are whole
Life
Essence
Being
Souls intertwine
Forever
And ever
Always
I am yours and you are mine

THANK YOU

Thank you so much for reading **Ink Veins**. If you wouldn't mind taking a moment to leave a review on the retailer site where you made your purchase, Goodreads, and/or BookBub it would mean the world to me.

Reviews help other readers find and enjoy the book too!

Much love,

Persephone

MORE BY PERSEPHONE

Broken Metronome

When the music of the heart dies…

Broken Metronome is an angsty poetry collection full of heartache and the possibility of what may have been.

Transcendental

A musician in search of his muse and a woman grieving the loss of her husband. Two weeks at an exclusive retreat and their connection rivals all others. Until she leaves early without notice. But he refuses to give up until he finds her again.

The Click Duet

High school sweethearts torn apart. When fate gives them a second chance, one doesn't trust they won't be hurt again. Through the Lens (Click Duet #1) and Time Exposure (Click Duet #2) is an angsty, second chance, friends to lovers romance with all the feels.

The Inked Duet

A man with a broken heart and a woman scared to put herself out there. Love is never easy. Sometimes love rips you apart. Fine Line (Inked Duet #1) and Love Buzz (Inked Duet #2) is a second chance at love, single parent romance with a pinch of angst and dash of suspense.

Distorted Devotion

Free-spirited Sarah lives life to the fullest. When a new love interest enters her life, she starts receiving strange gifts and letters. She doesn't want to relinquish her freedom or new love, but fears the consequences.

Undying Devotion

A long-term couple, Christy and Rick, live in a world of secrets. Their friends envy the bond they share, but remain oblivious to their lifestyle and how deep the bond lies. Until a turn of events has Christy wanting to open up.

Beloved Devotion

Liz asks the love of her life, Tiffany, to marry her. When Tiffany hesitates, but says yes, Liz is determined to learn why. As the pieces start to fall in place, Liz discovers she doesn't know her fiancée at all.

Depths Awakened

A small town romance which captivates you from the start. Mags and Geoff are two broken souls who have sworn off love. Vowed to never lose anyone else. But their undeniable attraction brings them together and refuses to let go.

CONNECT WITH PERSEPHONE

Connect with Persephone
www.persephoneautumn.com

Subscribe to Persephone's newsletter
www.persephoneautumn.com/newsletter

Join Persephone's reader's group
Persephone's Playground

Follow Persephone online

- instagram.com/persephoneautumn
- facebook.com/persephoneautumnwrites
- tiktok.com/@persephoneautumn
- goodreads.com/persephoneautumn
- bookbub.com/authors/persephone-autumn
- amazon.com/author/persephoneautumn
- pinterest.com/persephoneautumn
- twitter.com/PersephoneAutum

ACKNOWLEDGMENTS

Thank you to everyone who read through this vast collection of poetry. It means more than you know. Carving out pieces of yourself and putting them on paper for all to read is quite daunting.

Thank you to my amazing cover designer, Kat Savage, for creating the beautiful cover and the sectional art for the paperback. Everything you make is magical and wonderful and perfection.

Thank you to Ellie at My Brother's Editor for catching and fixing my boo boo's. Top-notch, rockstar status! You really are the best!

To every author and blogger and reader who promotes my work… the book community never ceases to amaze me.

And to myself… for being brave enough to expose such an intimate piece of myself to the world.

ABOUT THE AUTHOR

Persephone Autumn lives in Florida with her wife, crazy dog, and two lover-boy cats. A proud mom with a cuckoo grandpup. An ethnic food enthusiast who has fun discovering ways to veganize her favorite non-vegan foods. If given the opportunity, she would intentionally get lost in nature.

For years, Persephone did some form of writing; mostly journaling or poetry. After pairing her poetry with images and posting them online, she began the journey of writing her first novel.

She mainly writes romance, but on occasion dips her toes in other works. Look for her poetry publications and a psychological horror under P. Autumn.

Let Go

So much strength

So much fury

Let go of pain

Let go of worry

Allow love and light

Enter deep within

What's done is done

Tomorrow now begins

Lean over to your left

Lean back to your right

We are here for each other

To bid good morning and good night

Art of Geisha

Once a beautiful Maiko
Blooming, becoming Geisha
Years of transformation
Graceful artist, entertainer
Talent and tradition
Shamisen in her song
Elegant kimono, obi
Classical butō, eyes follow along
Artist, performer
How Geisha is defined
Entrancing those around her
Observing as they pined
Exotic, desired beauty
Versed with poetry and story
Dancing the words written
Geisha in all her glory

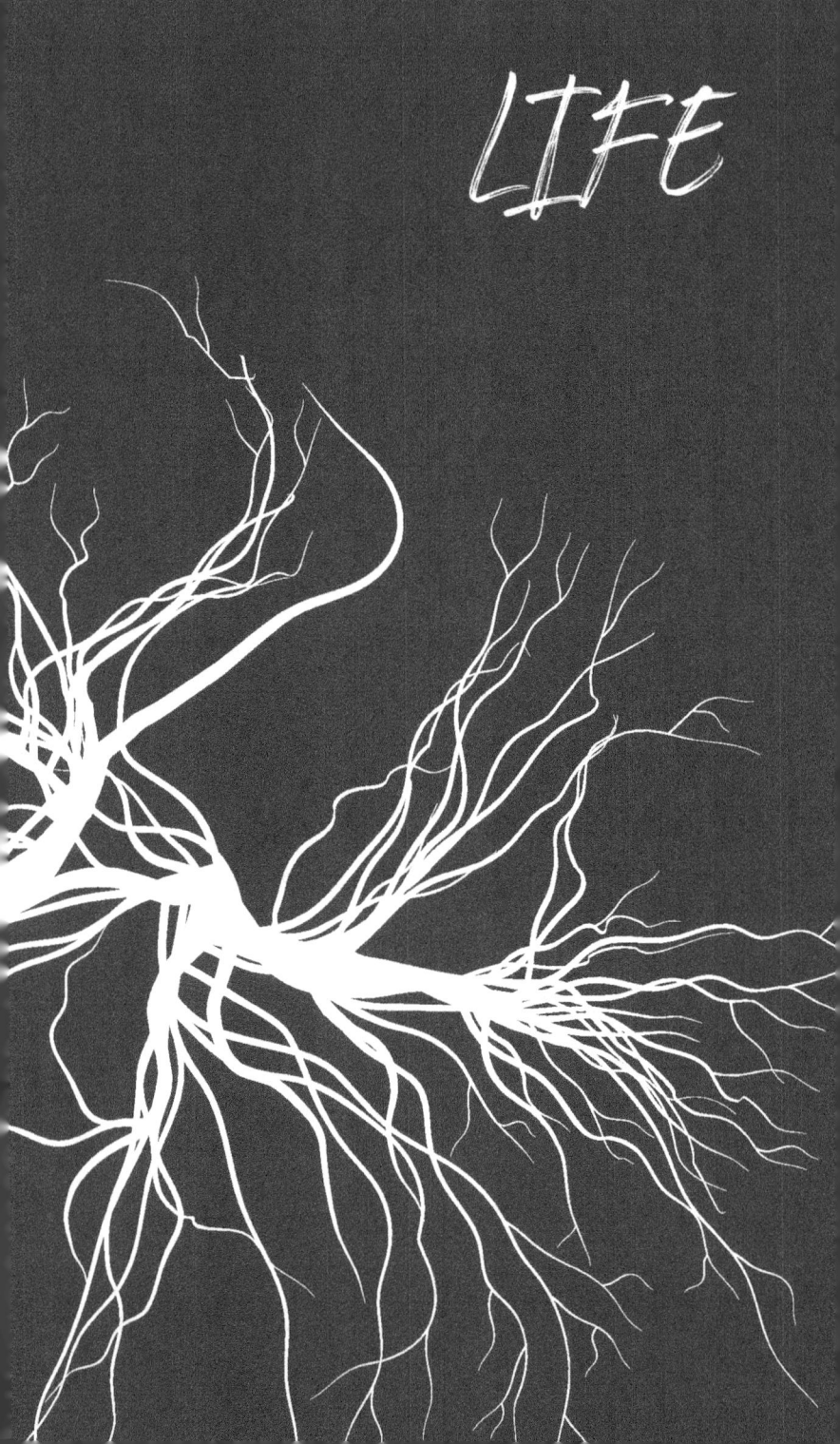

One touch
One taste
Instant addiction
Act without haste
Relentless pull
Draws us near
Magnetic
Electric
Neither having fear
Yank my ass
In the air
Wrapped around your wrist
Jerk my hair
Every inch
Own me whole
I give it all
Complete control
One touch
One taste
The primal beast
Inside awakes

primal

Lust

Interest
Intrigue
Fascination
Desire
Fantasy
Infatuation
Craving
Intensity
Undeniable
Yearning
Magnetic
LUST

Take hold
Grasp my flesh
Reel me in
Make us mesh
Feel my warmth
Make it rise
In the arch of my back
To the depths of my eyes
Skin on skin
Pulse pounding with mine
Synchronized bodies
Dancing in time
Sweat glistens
Seeping from pores
Moans cry out
Begging for more
Flipping, riding
Soaking the sheets
Sounds of lust
Ever increase
Apex fast approaches
Screaming for release
One last thrust
What each of us needs
Heads fall back
Panting for breath
Collapsing bodies
In need of rest
Take hold
Grasp me tight
Reel me in
Bid me goodnight

CUFFED

Here I stand
In patience and grace
Cuffs of pleasure
In their rightful place
Shoulders back
Hands in chaste
Eyes descending
Feel no haste
Ready, waiting
Pleasure consumes
Internal combustion
Anticipation for you

Marked

You want her
You've claimed her
Grab her hips
Go ahead, taste her
Lick her flesh
Bite her hard
Feel her tremble
Leave your mark
Make her moan
Make her shout
Be the man
She can't live without
Take her rough
Pull her hair
Make her feel it
Everywhere
Bind her hands
Hold her legs
Drive her intensely
Hear her beg
Grab her nipples
Squeeze them tight
Feel her clench
Bliss undenied
Seduce her mind
Feel her bare
Sing to her heart
No one will compare

Blindfolded

Eyes blanketed in darkness
Patiently awaiting her cue
Breath deepening, aroused
Pulse off-kilter, askew
His words seduce her mind
Elixir for her soul
Bound by a connection
She thought she'd never know
Passion set ablaze
Flesh heated with desire
Giving in to their every whim
Urges that never tire
Language all their own
No words need be spoken
Intertwined by divinity
World now awoken

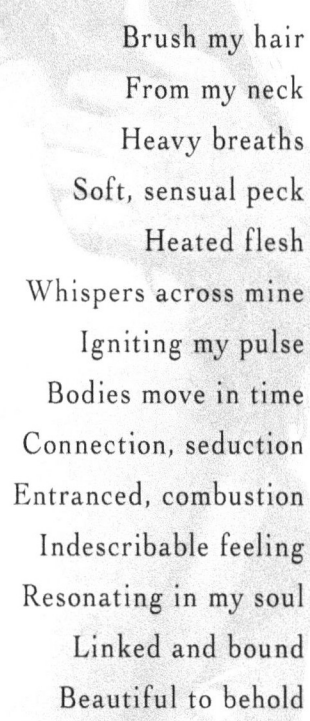

Brush my hair
From my neck
Heavy breaths
Soft, sensual peck
Heated flesh
Whispers across mine
Igniting my pulse
Bodies move in time
Connection, seduction
Entranced, combustion
Indescribable feeling
Resonating in my soul
Linked and bound
Beautiful to behold

Beholden

Wax Play

Intricate black lace
Invades her sight
Glowing warmth
Flickered candlelight
Anticipation
At growing heights
Slowly dripping
Waxed skin bites
Heavy sigh
Deeper gasp
Craving more
Gifted alas
Seduction and art
Paired into one
A give and take
Both come undone

You and Him and the Kiss

Lashes temporarily cast down
Slowly lifting
Eyes lock
Pulse flutters
Heat radiates
From every pore
Space closing between us
Time slows
Every molecule on fire
Lips graze
Asking permission
Another brush
More acceptance
Separation
Tongues tempt
Deeper invitations exchange
Hands grip hair
Pulling
Devouring
Breathless without care
Longing infinite seduction
The world absent
It is just you and him
And the kiss

Tangled Lovers

Dreaming of your body
Flesh against mine
Tangled limbs
Melting, intertwined
Your hand slowly moving
Caressing my breast
Arching, aching
Kissing tongues aggress
Hips buck, grind
Pleasurable pace
Empowered by desire
Pleasure written on your face
Not much longer
We shall come undone
A most beautiful ending
Exploding like the sun

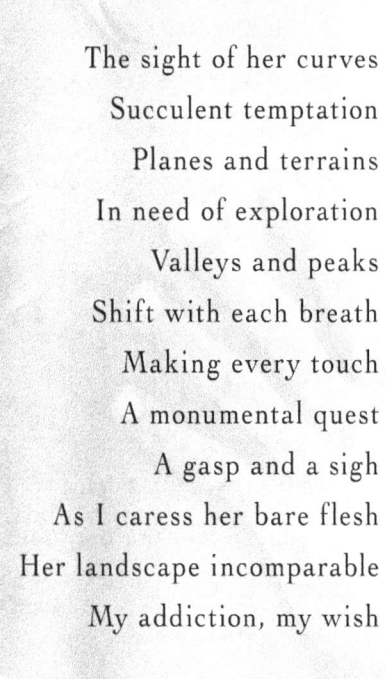

The sight of her curves
Succulent temptation
Planes and terrains
In need of exploration
Valleys and peaks
Shift with each breath
Making every touch
A monumental quest
A gasp and a sigh
As I caress her bare flesh
Her landscape incomparable
My addiction, my wish

Exploration

Endless Loop

Longing, burning
Aching, yearning
Grabbing, pulling
Embracing, lulling
Heating, kissing
Twining, blissing
Needing, filling
Moving, stilling
Sweating, breathing
Pulsing, heaving
Sating, feating
Loving, repeating

Fire and Ice

Fire and ice
Heated desire
She hides her lust
He pushes his pyre
Braced for impact
Ready to burn
Core driven purely
Two bodies link, churn
No way to distinguish
Ice or fire
Melted into one
Their unity we admire

our abyss

Smoothly we twirl
Into our own abyss
Plummeting deeper
Toward eternal bliss
Grasping and pulling
Never fulfilled
Indescribable need
Only one can still
Deep, enveloping
Swallowed in Earth
Radiating aura
Rapture gives birth

Naughty Dream

She dreamt a dream
A naughty spell
Awoke in lust
No one to tell
Heated and needing
Grabbing at sheets
Mad with desire
In need of release
Alone she starts
Visions fabricated in mind
Journey to euphoria
Passionately she will find

Everlasting Kiss

Lips yearning, aching
Deep soul scorching kiss
How you temp, tease me
Grazing my chin, lips
Soft, supple invitation
Open in a gasp
Shifted, heated posture
Tongue slips in at last
Dance of two lovers
Drown out the world
State of euphoria
Mind, body unfurled
How we each crave
Strong passionate lips
Melting us together
Everlasting kiss

Cravings

Cravings...
The feeling of your lips
Crushed against mine
The feeling of our hearts
Pulsing in time
The feeling of your fingers
Trace along my hips
The feeling as you trace
My body with your lips
Sudden rush of blood
Courses through my veins
Driving pure lust
Scorching sensual pains
Cravings buried within
Ever so deep
Awaken inner being
Wake up from your sleep

Photographer and the Model

Opportunity to capture
Her beauty, her essence
Black lace, seductive eyes
Defining her presence
Basking before him
Lens zooms, clicks
Voyeur arousal
Body heats, slicks
Passions flare
Flames of desire
Her body the torch
Setting his soul on fire

Forever Hers

Slight yet exquisite
Soft along her curves
A deep longing in her eyes
Yearning to be yours
Flowing full of mystery
Secrets behind her mask
Pent up desires aching
Blooming free at last
With one touch, one kiss
One sway of her hips
You're caught, in a trance
Forever hers, at every glance

Quake and Shiver

The simplest touch
Caress or timid feel
No comparison
To a lover's appeal
I quake and shiver
Hand glides low
Head tips back
Body begins to glow
Anticipation in the air
He whispers in my ear
"I want you now
I'm taking you. Here"

Given willingly
Heart and soul
Unwavering trust
Sir's complete control
Blindfolded eyes
Spread knees, straightened back
She waits endlessly
Anticipation intact
For Sir she will do
All that he asks
For she is submissive
At home, at last

Collared

Switch

Yielding strength
Courageous gift
Bowing before thee
Roles reverse, shift
A bold display
Not taken for granted
Elegant in form
Body enchanted
Release imminent
Quivering head to toe
Beauty of the switch
A fulfillment to bestow

Seductress

Curves so lush

Beckon me near

Ravenous desire

Drives me here

To touch

To smell

To taste

To hear

Blinded by seduction

Drawn to your skin

The sweet taste of your body

All over and again

Pinked Porcelain

Skin like porcelain
Soft and supple
Desire to touch
Almost unstoppable
Beautifully fragrant
Blossoms entangle
Caressing the senses
Enrapture enabled
Delicate is the beauty
Of such fair flesh
For the possibilities are endless
To pink with blemish

THE BURN

grab my hips

yank me back

now pull my hair

harder, like that

please quench

the burn

this is what

I yearn

loud gasp

deep sigh

that feeling

oh my...

Bound Ballerina

She dances in beauty
In elegance and grace
Twirling on toes
Dressed in lace
When the curtain falls
And one show ends
She bows her head
A new dance begins
She takes a step back
Her Sir takes the lead
He binds her in love
Everything she needs
Bound by passion
Consumed with taste
For her Master
Love will never waste

This is for Me

I surrender myself
Unto you
Chained and bound
What will you do
At your mercy
Trust instilled
Anticipation
Half the thrill
Head back
Eyes closed
Awaiting my Master
Fully exposed
Deep breath in
Contented sigh out
Fingers graze my flesh
Shivers run about
No other place
I would rather be
Words whispered
"This is for me"

His Knots, My Binds

Knots
Binds
Of rope
Is mine
Trust
Surrender
Heart
I render
Give
Receive
Love
Achieve
I trust
He decides
His knots
My binds

Driving Me Wild

The scent of her skin
Driving me wild
Her salty sweet flesh
My tongue strokes for miles
Following her curves
Delectable hips
Tongue tracing up
Those voluptuous tits
Peaks and valleys
I pause to admire
Then resume my discovery
Licking along my desire
All hot and bothered
She makes me pulse hard
Uncontrollably wet
Fingers sliding along
Her back arches deep
Body melting slow
Sinking teeth in
She loses all control

Wet Apparition

Slowly appearing to me
Apparition of the night
Surrounded in smoke
Heart soaring to flight
I close my eyes
Awaken thoughts, mind
Visions temptation
My body comes alive
I jolt to alert
Lost
Aroused
Shaken
Only the imagination
Mind
Body
Soul awaken

Flesh Keys

He touched her flesh
Unadulterated control
Lilting her song
Playing the melody of her soul
Aching for more
His hands glided over the keys
Stroking all the notes
Her body rises with pleas
Only one set of hands
Ignites her symphony within
Performing her melody
Over and over again

SEDUCTION

life stolen

Unsettling winds
Carry the essence of fear
Stirring at the core
Buzzing chaos within the mind
Clarity
Tampering with the soul
Tearing
Burning
Depleting everything known
Churn the scorching embers
Residual moments stolen
Plummet into the abyss
Forever lost
Life stolen

Tortured Soul

The tortured soul...
One that can see the light
But focuses on the dark
Wears the expression of joy
But screams sadness in the mind
Ensures the happiness of others
While forgetting what it is to have their own
Usually sits in the corner alone
Secretly desiring the attention of others
Is praised for their greatness
Yet feels no purpose
Loves unconditionally
Although often in the aura of neglect
Silently gasping
Attracting rescue
Aspirations for strength
Fantasizing of hope

Believe Nothing Less

Poison seeping through my veins
Toxic and raping my mind
Abducting my sanity
Bit by bit
Replaced with insecurities
Self doubt
Knowing my thoughts are skewed
Telling myself they are false
Yet still toxicity wars with me
As if on a mission of mercy
Pulling me under its wing
Making me feel inadequate
I close my eyes and whisper...
I am beautiful
I am worthy
I am desirable
Believe nothing less
Don't allow your mind to create falsehoods that
slowly torment and taunt
The past does not dictate the present
Nor the future
I do
I am strong
Even when I am weak and frail

a hindrance
a bother
a disruption like any other
a nuisance
a pest
a soul never at rest

Watch Me Bleed

Take my tongue
Rendered mute
Now you'll never hear
All my truths
Pretty penny
On the floor
Not worth the time
Not anymore
Slit my throat
Watch me bleed
It doesn't matter
An absent dream

The Thorn

A thorn

Prick

Poke

Stab

Too much

A droplet forming

Not enough

Pooling

Overbearing

Dripping

In your face

Pouring

Out of the way

Puddling

Cracked shell

Paling

Shattered

Falling

Broken

Comatose

Defeated

A ghost

Ghostly Existence

Seconds drag out

Twisting into minutes

Piling up

Weighing down

Clumping into hours

Days

Swallowing whole

Deep

Deep

Into the fissures of my soul

Ripping me

Shredding me

Tearing me

Limb from limb

Until nothing remains

Until a faint memory

A ghost

Is all that exists

weakling

mute
words don't matter

listen
only hear what does

quiet
your voice is an irritant

absence
the best solution

cower
all that is left

shrivel
a cornered weakling

disappear
a glint in time

gone
inevitability

g r a s p i n g   f o r   a n y o n e

Stop it
No more
That's enough
Be done
Help me
Slipping
Sinking
Drowning
Breathless
Pulsing
Pounding
Gasping
Reaching
Pleading
For someone
Anyone
Who matters

A Shadow in the Moonlight

It's not the darkness which frightens me
But the light illuminating every corner
The dark is my shelter
And the light an amplifier
There is something to be said
About someone who hides in themselves
Peace and madness
Quiet and screams
All the things that haunt
Not only your dreams
The light is not safe
Not from others
Your deepest thoughts and emotions
A love letter to strangers
I do not fear the dark
And not prefer the light
If forced to choose
I'd be a shadow in the moonlight

VACANT DREAM

It doesn't matter what I say
It doesn't matter what I do
It doesn't matter how hard I try
I can never please you
I try my damnedest
Fill myself with strength
But when it comes down to it
I am never enough
I'm just a sad, lonely soul
Weaving my way through life
Wishing for someone
Consider my trial
I feel like I'm running
Trying to catch up
Wishing I could be the one
You want to give attention to
At times I feel lost
Frozen runner up
Not the first choice
No matter what
I want to be touched
I want to be seen
I want to be loved
Not someone's vacant dream

Restart

I feel so lost
Like crying all the time
No reason in particular
Just sadness
I want to do nothing
To be nothing
I want peace
Silence
Darkness
Solitude
I crave serenity
Beauty
Sanity
I ponder the inevitable
Question who I am
Question what to do
If I were words on a chalkboard
I would ask to be erased
Maybe, just maybe
To start again

NEEDS

I need your smile
So that I can smile too
I need your comfort
To relieve my painful wounds
I need you...
And perhaps
You need me too

SHUNNED

Shunned was all she felt
Darkness like a disease
Drowning, suffocating her
No one heard her pleas
Beauty was a gift
Her eyes could never see
Tragedy was her curse
All she felt she would ever be
Hearts only quest
Find what is yours
Shed no more tears
Walk your destiny, walk your course

Black to Hue

Pondering, questing
Thirst of knowledge grows
Hungry for answers
Questions won't flow
Gaze into the distance
Eyes in a haze
Mind becomes empty
Memory ablaze
Temporary sadness
Sways forth and back
Close out the world
My insides go black
Relief to be found
Simple and true
Awaiting sounds and feelings
Turning black another hue

Mascara Streaks

Soulful eyes full
Seeking to release
Sorrow, yet joy
Hidden no one sees
Sudden rush inside
Crushing in my chest
Shove away the hurt
Let it go, retain happiness
Be bold, be strong
You're beautiful, you belong
Be who you are, forget hate
Strength in love, never dissipate

Angel of Death

A gasp for breath
Unable to take
Beating in her chest
A slowing fate
Red splayed around her
In beauty like a gown
Essence of her soul
Seeping to surround
With eyes lightly focused
Ears with no sound
Dark beauty appeared before her
Lowering to the ground
Beauty whispered in her ear
"All will be alright,
Just close your eyes, my love
And know you are now mine"

To Feel Alive

In darkness and light
I tread softly out of sight
Eyes averted most often
Sounds slowly soften
Busy mind attempts solace
Visions diminish promise
Unwavering senses gruff
Question am I enough
Pacing along the earth
Seeking out my worth
Lost amongst the trees
Hidden within the seas
Treasure cannot be found
For who will it astound
Senses in overdrive
Aspiring to feel alive

Drained

Language sparsely stated
Mind shutting down
Attempted alleviation
Effort lost for sound
Sadness crawling through my veins
Weaving its worrisome web
Draining away my being
Bleeding through thoughts unsaid
Bottom of the totem
A passing thought in the wind
Water rolling downward
What a world we live in

Lost

Lost

In my own head

In my own heart

At a loss

Morality out the window

Esteem out the door

Wandering

Scanning the earth for a clue

Guidance evading every move

Lost

Walking aimlessly

Reacting erratically

Detachment

Disconnected
Feeling detached from life
Alternative
First place in strife
Backup
Illusion is the foreground
Appointed
Animated in the background
Withdrawal
Hibernating amongst the cold
Epilogue
The path till gray and old

Live or Dream

At times, the world is shrouded in darkness
At times, there is no light
So many times, there is hopelessness
Every day feels like it is night
A smile plastered across your cheeks
A nod to signal you are fine
Disguising how you truly feel
Your brain screaming inside
The weight of the world
So heavy in your chest
The burdens you keep within
You save from the rest
A battle of one waging war
Your mind fracturing at the seams
The most challenging decision to make
Do I live or settle in dreams

not her

I cannot be her
Not my eyes
Not my hair
Not my face
Not my body

I cannot be her
Not my humor
Not my intelligence
Not my tears
Not my pain

I cannot be her
Not my laughter
Not my happiness
Not my pleasure
Not my kindness

I cannot be her
I am not her
I will never be her
Nor do I want to be

I cannot be her
I am simply me
Broken
Small
Shy
Meek

Love me for me
For I can only be me

SORROW

INTRODUCTION

Ink Veins is a collection of poetry written over the span of a decade.

Several of the poems in this collection were written to images I found on the internet. Images that inspired me or I found a certain beauty in.

Other poems in the collection are written from pure emotion. Honestly, the sadder the poem, the likelier it is I wrote it during a dark time.

For me, poetry only calls at certain times. It isn't something I set out to write. And the likelihood of frequent collections is rare. My goal is to create a new collection every one to two years. Although, they will not be as large as this.

I hope you enjoy Ink Veins.

To all the people out there who feel everything.

Who trudge through the darkest hours and land in the brightest days.

The ones who fantasize and lead a double life in their mind.

This is for you…

Insomniac Duet

Restless Night

A Love So Bright

Poetry Collections

Ink Veins

Broken Metronome

Standalone Horror Novels

By Dawn (published under P. Autumn)

BOOKS BY PERSEPHONE AUTUMN

Standalone Romance Novels

Depths Awakened

Sweet Tooth

Transcendental

Devotion Series

Distorted Devotion

Undying Devotion

Beloved Devotion

Darkest Devotion

Bay Area Duet Series

Click Duet

Through the Lens

Time Exposure

Inked Duet

Fine Line

Love Buzz

Ink Veins

Copyright © 2020 by Persephone Autumn

www.persephoneautumn.com

All rights reserved.

No part of this book may be reproduced in any form or by any electronic or mechanical means, including photocopying, information storage and retrieval systems, without written permission from the author except for the use of brief quotations in a book review.

This book is a work of fiction. Names, characters, establishments, organizations, and incidents are either products of the author's imagination or are used fictitiously to give a sense of authenticity. Any resemblance to actual events, places, or persons, living or dead, is entirely coincidental.

If you're reading this book and did not purchase it, or it was not purchased for your use only, or it was purchased on a site I do not advertise I sell on, then it was pirated illegally. Please purchase a copy of your own on a platform where the author advertises she distributes and respect the hard work of this author.

ISBN: 978-1-951477-06-6 (Ebook)

ISBN: 978-1-951477-07-3 (Paperback)

Editor: Ellie McLove | My Brother's Editor

Cover Design: Kat Savage | Kat Savage Designs

INK VEINS

PERSEPHONE AUTUMN

BETWEEN WORDS PUBLISHING LLC